MW00911542

MY OTHER MOTHERS

BY CHRISTINE CLARK

5/27/19

My Dearest Jack,

My Other Mothers

A Memoir

Christine Clark

Thank you for
encouraging and supporting
me in my writing
endeavors — and having
faith in me!

Love Always,
Chris

For Helen Brahmstadt Dorner

1909 – 2010

EACH OF US CAN LOOK BACK UPON SOMEONE WHO MADE A GREAT
DIFFERENCE IN OUR LIVES, SOMEONE WHOSE WISDOM OR SIMPLE ACTS
OF CARING MADE AN IMPRESSION UPON US. IN ALL LIKELIHOOD IT WAS
SOMEONE WHO SOUGHT NO RECOGNITION FOR THEIR DEED OTHER THAN
THE JOY OF KNOWING THAT, BY THEIR HAND,
ANOTHER'S LIFE HAD BEEN MADE BETTER.

STEPHEN M. WOLF
PROMINENT AMERICAN BUSINESS EXECUTIVE

My Other Mothers

I Have Lost the Ring

I have lost the ring—the ring my godmother gave me. It was her birthstone, a peridot, a yellow gemstone set in a beautiful 1950s-era setting. It was worth no more than a few hundred dollars, but it was invaluable to me in sentiment and meaning. The loss of this ring has evoked many memories of growing up in the 1940s and 1950s—especially my memories of the women who became "my other mothers" during the times when my own mother was unavailable to me.

My mother, Helen Dorner, was certainly a loving and caring woman and mother. But, the pressures of having a second child, my sister Linda, together with the fact that my dad, Edward Dorner, was often away because of work, meant that my mother was sometimes overwhelmed and welcomed the respite of having me spend time with friends and family. She needed the break.

Besides my godmother, these women also included a cherished neighbor, two teachers and a Navy wife. I neither had nor have any bad feelings toward my mother about this. I certainly understand the work it takes to raise children, sometimes by oneself, and I know that my mother did her absolute best for me. In many important ways, my life was enriched by the time spent with these women. I can't help but look fondly at that time in my life, which is why I've written this book. I'm certain that my extended family, friends and other readers will understand my point of view. One's life moves along many paths. It's the journey, in all its parts, that is important.

Now, back to the ring—the ring I lost three years ago during a big transition in my life. I had downsized from a twelve-room house where I had lived since 1981. My husband, Tom, had passed away seven years prior to this move, and I had decided to turn over my house to my daughter, Katy, her husband Carlo and their two boys, Teagan and Jared.

Somewhere during the summer of the move into my new living space, the ring disappeared.

As sad as I was over its loss, I was inspired to write about my god-mother and the other women I knew growing up and how they influenced my life. Not only were they there for me when I needed them, but they influenced me in many life-changing decisions—to get a college education, to marry a good and decent man and to have children of my own, as four of my "other mothers" had done.

They enriched my life. I believe other women have also been inspired by special women in their growing-up years, as I was. I was fortunate to have had "other mothers" in my own life.

MY OTHER MOTHERS

CHRISTINE LOGSDON

My first "other mother" was Christine Logsdon, who was my god-mother. I must have been named after her. We called her Aunt Sis. She was born Christine Virginia Crist in 1906 in a log house on a farm in

Hinton in Rockingham County, Virginia. She was the third child and first daughter of a family of nine children. The family moved several times and eventually settled in Rockville, Maryland. In 1927, at age twenty, Christine entered the Emergency Hospital Training School for Nurses in Washington, D.C. It was during this time that she met her husband, DeEarle Logsdon. Years later, she documented her life in her autobiography, *Sunrise—Sunset*.

She published this memoir in 1985, and I have read this fascinating story more than once. Her husband, DeEarle, and my father were class-mates at the United States Naval Academy, Class of 1930. In her book, Aunt Sis describes how she met her future husband:

> An old beau, Lenford Miller, from the Shenandoah Valley came down to see me [in Rockville]. I had al-ready declined his first proposal before we left the val-ley. I told him that I was too young and wanted more schooling. On one particular evening, we took the trolley to Glen Echo Amusement Park outside of Washington, D.C. We were sitting on a bench by the merry-go-round when my brother Howard walked up with a handsome young man in the white uniform of a U.S. Coast Guard officer. His name was DeEarle Logsdon, the man I later married. I think Lenford and I knew when I met DeEarle that marriage was not for us.

3

Because Dad and DeEarle were classmates—when my parents eventually moved to the Washington, D.C., area, and later when Linda, my younger sister and I were growing up—we socialized with the Logsdons as families. Aunt Sis came into my life when they were living on a small farm in Annandale, Virginia, located on Little River Road. Little River was a stream that ran through the woods on the back half of their property. There she raised vegetables, berries, chickens, guinea hens and rabbits. A visit to their farm was an adventure, as her son Chip and my sister Linda and I would roam the property, stirring up excitement in the hen house by yelling and flapping our arms up and down, crossing the creek by walking on a large log, watching the rabbits in their hutches and, at the end of the day, enjoying a homemade dinner consisting entirely of food raised on their mini-farm. We dined on roast guinea hen, green beans, tomatoes and lettuce from the garden, fresh corn on the cob and, for dessert, apple or berry pie, topped with a dollop of ice cream. What yummy fare! While Aunt Sis enjoyed her country life working on "the farm," DeEarle commuted to Washington where he worked as a lawyer for the U.S. government.

My godmother was beautiful, as Mom and Dad commented many times—a strawberry blonde with a flawless "peaches and cream" complexion and a trim and fit body, maintained, I am sure, by her active lifestyle. She was able to have only one child, Chip, who was born when his dad was away in the Navy during World War II. So although she had many nieces, I believe she thought of me as a daughter, and, thus, I got the ring.

My godmother filled in for my mother when I attended Camp High Road, a Methodist church camp in rural Virginia. I was ten years old, and it was my second time at the camp, as I had attended for one week the previous summer. Aunt Sis was the camp nurse, and, in that capacity, was able to rescue me when I became severely constipated because of my aversion to using the outdoor latrines! She moved me from the cabin I was sharing with other girls into the nurse's cabin with indoor plumbing. There she brought me back to good health with nutritious food and much tender care. This particular camp experience of sleeping in cabins without indoor plumbing made me realize that "roughing it" was not my style. I avoided similar camps in the future. But more importantly, I learned to appreciate my godmother even more, as she so lovingly cared for me during my brief illness.

As a teenager, I remember a wonderful weekend in the country with Mom, Aunt Sis, Linda, and a close girlfriend. It was October and a time to attend the Waterford Fair. Located near Leesburg, Virginia, this fair is still held today—as Linda and I revisited it one sweltering autumn day, three years ago. The town and the fair were much smaller in the 1950s and I remember a big cauldron of apple butter simmering in a street of this quaint community founded by Quakers in the 1700s. Walking around the cobblestone streets, we saw craftsmen exhibiting their wares, and, as the morning hours turned to noon, we walked to the small old Methodist church, where we had a delicious lunch of ham sandwiches and homemade apple pie, washed down with a cup of strong coffee.

Later that day, so long ago, we drove to our country place at the Shenandoah Retreat, along the Shenandoah River. Mom and Dad had a weekend cottage located on a small country road nestled among other similar cottages. This and other rural roads bordered the retreat, which consisted of a nine-hole golf course, a clubhouse and a man-made lake for swimming. In later years a swimming pool was built, as the lake was no longer safe for swimming. What caused the lake to be unsafe is a bit unclear, but possibly pollution—or the snakes in the water, sometimes seen along the far edge of the lake. The clubhouse was a mansion formerly owned by the Parker family. Its fame came from one of the owners, Judge Parker. Standing on the front lawn of the mansion, the Judge read the sentence condemning John Brown to death for his part in leading the failed raid on the United States Armory in nearby Harper's Ferry in 1859, one of the significant events that led to the Civil War. This property is located in the northern part of Virginia, between Leesburg and Winchester.

We spent the night in our cottage after our day at the Waterford Fair. I will always remember the dinner we shared that Mom had brought with us to heat up later that evening. Sitting at the table after dinner, the conversation turned to Aunt Sis' experiences at nursing school. Soon we were doubled over laughing, as she told stories of her days as a student—dating doctors, her experiences as a probationer (the first six months of nursing school spent entirely attending classes), embarrassing events she encountered and some stories that were quite "racy." That evening I felt that I was entering a new phase in my own life as a member of the grown-up community of women. I also saw another facet of my mother, as she laughed at these stories along with the rest of us. As my teen years continued, I realized my mother was no prude and was able to understand and support me in many of my new experiences.

Aunt Sis was part of a group of friends who gave me a bridal shower the summer before I got married. Her smiling face appears in my wedding photos.

Because my husband, Tom Clark, had been a lieutenant in the United States Army Corps of Engineers, our reception was at the Fort Myer Officers Club in Arlington, Virginia. Since I have already written about our exciting and romantic—some might say whirlwind—courtship and marriage in my memoir, *Letters from Berlin*, I won't go into detail here, except to say that I could not have been a happier bride on that beautiful day.

When it was time to leave the reception for our honeymoon, I had changed into my going-away outfit in the dressing room—and Aunt Sis came in carrying a small white hobnail china pot and saucer filled with Christmas holly to give me before I left. She gave me a hug which was the last hug I got from "family" before leaving with Tom. Mom and Dad were nowhere to be seen. They were downstairs, socializing with the wedding guests.

A year and a half later, I was visiting my family in Arlington, Virginia. I was expecting our first child. Tom and I were preparing to leave our home in Boston and move to Baden, Switzerland, where we would remain for one and a half years and where our son Paul would be born. At the time, Tom was working as an engineer for Allis-Chalmers Manufacturing Company in Hyde Park, Massachusetts. He was going to Baden to work with the Brown-Boveri Manufacturing Company, an international company which manufactured equipment for the electrical-power industry. Tom would work there in the Engineering Department adapting switchgear for use in the United States. It was an excellent opportunity for him career-wise, and, later, the contacts he made during this time enabled him to establish his own company in the Boston area in 1973.

Getting back to our time in Arlington Forest, before we left for Europe, Aunt Sis came to visit one afternoon. She laughed at me as she rubbed her hand over my protruding belly, which I had tried to conceal in my home-sewn navy blue "tent" maternity dress. Maternity clothes were so very different from today's styles, where expectant mothers now wear more revealing and stylish clothes, unabashedly proud of their condition!

Of course Aunt Sis was overjoyed for me and my impending motherhood. I look back on this time in wonder, as I was twenty-two years old, about to fly off to Europe and have my first child. Oh, the feelings of being invincible at that age. I believed I could do anything—even having my first child in a foreign country, far away from family and friends. But, of course, Tom was my family then.

At some point while Tom and I were living in Switzerland, Aunt Sis and DeEarle sold their mini-farm in Annandale and relocated to Florida. They lived in Seminole, in the central part of the state. Every year I received a Christmas card from her with vivid descriptions of their new life in sunny Florida—fishing near their home and having other Florida adventures.

After DeEarle passed away, Aunt Sis moved back to the Philadelphia area to be near her son, Chip, and his wife. Mom was unable to locate her, although she tried many times. In recent years, Linda and I drove to Annandale to find the site of the Logsdon home on Little River Road. Many condos and apartments now sit on what was once their rural property. We parked the car, got out and walked around. Suddenly, there it was—a street sign with the name "Logsdon Way." In the distance we saw and heard the water—yes, it was Little River.

I have lost the ring. I am sad. It was my connection to Christine Logsdon, "Aunt Sis," my dear godmother. Even more, it was my connection to my past and my youth. I feel somewhat disloyal. She entrusted her ring to me and I lost it. I still have the saucer from the white pot she gave me, but not the holly. Oh, but I have the memories.

My Other Mothers

My Neighborhood

So many memories of this time growing up have connections to my dad's ties to the United States Naval Academy. DeEarle was just one of Dad's many classmates from his Class of 1930. Growing up, I remember so well sitting on the steps leading upstairs at our house in Arlington Forest, watching the adults at my parents' many dinner parties. These guests were classmates from the Academy and their wives. I watched, enchanted, taking in the ladies' stylish cocktail dresses. I remember one lady wearing a deep-red-colored cocktail dress with matching high-heeled shoes. In those days, everybody smoked, the women often holding long cigarette holders while they slowly blew out wisps of smoke. This often added a touch of glamor, imitating the movie stars of the 40s —perhaps Bette Davis or Hedy Lamarr. I tried to catch bits of conversation buzzing through our living room before the guests began to slowly meander into the dining room. There, Mom had set up dinner on a long buffet table and guests would gather at smaller card tables to eat. After everyone had exited the living room, I would wander around peering into empty glasses, searching for abandoned maraschino cherries to eat. Of course, they were soaked in the dregs of various cocktails. Amazingly, I never became sick from these, as I must have sensed when to stop. I was always interested in what adults were doing and talking about. I was continually adding to my own index of important information!

Washington, D.C., was an interesting place to grow up. Mom would often tell me, "You will never live in another place like this." Although I love the Boston area where I have lived for over fifty years, from time to time I still talk to Mom, even though she is deceased: "Mom, you were so right." When I would visit her at Leisure World, a retirement community in Wheaton, Maryland, and then later at Vantage House, a continuous-care facility in Columbia, Maryland, we would talk about living in the Washington area. I would tell her that she was right about how interesting it was.

Then she would say to me, "But Tom took you away from here."

Then I would answer, "But, Mom, I wanted to go!"

Why was this area so interesting? As a child there were so many exciting places to see. One of my favorite places to visit was the Washington Monument. It was so much fun to ride the elevator to the top and look out over the city. In summertime, the Fourth of July fireworks were held on the Monument grounds, and Dad would take me every year. We would sit on folding wooden chairs at the foot of the monument and patiently wait through the music, speeches and other filler activities leading up to the big event—the fireworks!

One year, the popular crooner, Eddie Fisher, then in the military, sang during these activities. I am sure the song, "Oh! My Papa" was among the numbers he performed.

Another favorite Washington, D.C., attraction was the U. S. Botanic Garden; and trips there inspired my love of plants and gardening. I can still smell the rich damp muskiness of the gardens and see the various tropical plants growing up to the top of the high glass ceilings of the building.

Mom also took me to Sunday children's concerts at the National Symphony Orchestra, which I really enjoyed. Equally amazing were our trips to the Smithsonian museums. One of my favorite things to see was the display of the presidents' wives' inaugural-ball dresses in the American History Museum; I also loved the display of pianos from all different historical periods. Later I remember Whistler's Peacock Room at the Freer Gallery, also part of the Smithsonian. Sometimes Mom would take me for lunch at the United States Senate Restaurant where we would eat their special Senate Navy Bean Soup.

At Christmas time we would go to the Woodworth & Lothrop department store or, as we then called it, "Woodies," to see the windows all decorated for Christmas. When I was three, four, and five, we would eat in the Children's Dining Room at "Woodies." Poor Mom—it was tough for her to sit, as the tables and chairs were quite low to the floor, as they were designed for small children. I wonder how she maneuvered in a dress and high-heeled shoes—not to mention she had to eat the small, made-for-children menu offerings!

Later in my growing-up years, there were visits to the National Cathedral; the huge Mormon church; Lee Mansion, now called Arlington House; Arlington National Cemetery with the Tomb of the Unknown Soldier; and Mount Vernon along the Potomac River. Then there were summer vacation trips when we drove all over the state of Virginia, visiting Williamsburg; Jamestown; Stratford Hall, where Robert E. Lee was born; and Wakefield, birthplace of George Washington. The list goes on and on to include Civil War battlefields and birthplaces of famous presidents.

Today I feel blessed that Mom and Dad settled in Washington. What forces were in play to land them there? It was the trees! They both grew up in Crete, Nebraska. There were few trees in that part of eastern Nebraska.

In 1930, Mom visited Dad for June Week at the Naval Academy in Annapolis. Taking the train from Crete to Washington, D.C., and then from there riding the trolley to Annapolis, Mom saw trees lining the trolley tracks, trees overhanging the tracks—so many trees—trees she had never seen the likes of in Crete. I believe that day Mom fell in love with the East Coast.

My parents got married in 1933 and later settled in an apartment in Washington, and, as Mom told me many times, it was important to have the "right address." In 1934 one of these addresses was the Sixteenth Street area of the city. Eventually they moved to Arlington, living in several different garden apartments. One of the apartment complexes they lived in was Buckingham, which later plays an important role in my story during the time I was in elementary school.

While living there, one morning my mother heard a commotion just outside of the first-floor window. Looking out, she saw Eleanor Roosevelt standing among a gaggle of reporters, talking about the apartment complex! Buckingham was among the first, large-scale, housing developments in the country.

Here is a little bit of history, taken from a *Washington Post* article dated April 6, 2017, by Harriet Edleson:

> Much of the housing in the neighborhood was built be-
> ginning in 1936, and is part of the garden-apartment
> complex completed between 1937 and 1953 by Allie S.
> Freed, Clarence Stein and Henry Wright, who had
> founded Paramount Communities in 1935, and devel-
> oped the garden-apartment complex. Company president
> Freed owned Paramount Motors, a taxi manufacturer,
> and was chairman of the Committee for Economy
> Recovery and an associate of President Franklin D.
> Roosevelt. Stein was a developer, and Wright, a propo-
> nent of the Garden City movement, was the planner and
> architect. Market-rate loans from the New Deal's Federal
> Housing Authority financed much of the Buckingham
> Community's development according to the neighbor-
> hood conservation plan.

The now-historic garden apartment achieved local and national recognition on that day, witnessed by my mother, when First Lady Eleanor Roosevelt visited and commented in her daily "My Day" column:

> It is a delightful development....well planned...gives
> one a feeling that there is a possibility of doing many
> things on a community basis that would make life easier
> for the individual family.

After leaving Buckingham, Mom and Dad moved to another garden-apartment complex, Arlington Village in South Arlington. Finally, in March of 1941, they bought our house in Arlington Forest, the house where I lived from the moment I came home from George Washington

University Hospital as a newborn in November, 1941, until I married at age twenty-one and left.

Arlington Forest was developed in 1941, the first houses being built prior to the war, and later sections were finished after the war. Our home was located at 113 North Columbus Street, part of the first stage of this complex. This area was developed on land purchased from the Henderson Estate. The estate was a hunting lodge belonging to the Henderson family who had a large home in Washington D.C., referred to as "Henderson Castle." During the war, the Arlington property lodge was used as an officers' club. It later burned down, consumed by a fast-moving fire, when I was ten years old. As a child, I remember walking to the former lodge and being intrigued by its past.

Part of this wonderful neighborhood was a natural centerpiece, Lubber Run Park, which ran parallel to our street. The park also separated the streets and houses of Arlington Forest built on either side of it. It was not uncommon to describe where a friend lived as "on the other side of the park." The park was formed from what looks like an enormous gorge, probably created from some sort of geologic disturbance eons earlier.

Lubber Run Creek, a rapidly flowing body of water, ran the entire length of the park, finally entering a culvert, becoming much deeper, and leaving the park as it disappeared under Route 50. Spanning the creek from the paths that bordered it on each side were wooden bridges with railings. Standing on the bridges and looking down, we could see and hear the rushing water as it splashed against the broken glacial rocks of the creek bed, as well as against the rocks along both sides of the creek. We would access the park from the various public entrances or just by running down the hills of neighbors' back yards. Whenever I return to the "old neighborhood" I re-visit the park. As I walk down the path at the main entrance, I immediately smell the creek. This smell is unlike any I have experienced in New England where I have lived for over fifty years. The creek smell assails the senses. It is pungent, earthy, and dank—but, oh, the memories it evokes! Memories of crossing the creek on the wooden bridges, memories of wading barefoot with the neighborhood boys who caught crayfish from the creek bed, or memories of summer picnics in the park, staying until dark when the mosquitos forced us to climb the path and return home.

Growing up in Arlington Forest was an education in itself. Among the residents were military officers and their families, government employees from all parts of the United States, as well as just regular folks —store owners, teachers and people who did not move away!

Living on our street were many distinguished people. There was Colonel Jack Hilger, United States Air Force. Colonel Hilger flew in Jimmy Doolittle's raid over Tokyo. In fact, he was second-in-command during the raid. Colonel Charles T. (Buck) Lanham, United States Army, and his family lived down the street from us. Colonel Lanham was a war-time friend of Ernest Hemingway. After the war, Hemingway came to visit his old friend. Mom and other neighbors were "blown away" by this neighborhood event. Another military family down the street were the Rostows—Colonel Rostow, United States Army, and his wife and children. The rumor was that Rostow's wife was related to General Ulysses S. Grant. Once a month a large black limousine would arrive in front of the house, and a dowager dressed entirely in black, wearing a black veil, would emerge to visit her great-granddaughter. Also living on our street was a family of German-Jewish refugees, the Hokes. The parents were both physicians—but they could not practice medicine in the United States, because of regulations at the time. They had two teenage children, Axel and René, whom I liked to visit when I was six and seven. I later wondered why they were so nice to me! I had free access to the upstairs of their house and I would ask them so many questions! Across the street and next door to the Hokes were the Brusslers. They were Germans as well, refugees from post-World War I. They had one daughter, Hildegarde, and two dogs. The garden behind their house was terraced and descended down toward Lubber Run Park. It was beautiful and was lovingly and painstakingly cared for by Mr. Brussler. He was a grouchy sort of man, but Dad had a soft spot in his heart for him; in fact, every Christmas, Dad took me over to the Brusslers to have a glass of wine with Mr. Brussler. I did not like the wine. It was too sweet!

The neighborhood was a fascinating place. I loved to watch the military officers, dressed in their uniforms walking down the street on their way to the bus stop located at the shopping center behind our house. The uniforms were two toned—tan pants and dark-brown jackets. It was just after the end of the Second World War and these men were mostly stationed at the Pentagon, which Dad referred to as "The Squirrel Cage." Another family lived across the street; the Hanburgers. Colonel Hanburger was U.S. Army and also stationed at the Pentagon. He later went to Korea during the Korean conflict. Their children were Chris, my age, and Susan, my sister's age. We became great pals. Chris played football at Hampton High School in Hampton, Virginia, then joined the Army. Later he went to the University of North Carolina on a football scholarship. He was drafted by the Washington Redskins as a linebacker and was a star player for them for his entire career. In 2011 he was elected to the Pro Football Hall of Fame.

Chris was a sort of celebrity in the Washington area as an adult and appeared in various television commercials. When the Hanburgers first moved in, I was almost seven and about to enter the second grade. The parents were there, but the children were still with their grandparents in South Carolina. Mrs. Hanburger, Sis, as she was called (another "Sis"), was gardening in her front yard, pulling weeds, and performing other landscaping projects to beautify the property. I decided to go over and introduce myself and proceeded to tell her all about the neighborhood and the residents. She seemed interested in my stories, but the next day Mom went over to apologize for my intrusion.

"Oh no," Mrs. Hanburger replied, "I didn't mind at all. It was really interesting to hear about our new neighborhood and all of the neighbors."

ENTERING THE KITCHEN

So, now that I have tried to give an accurate description of my neighborhood when I was a child, I will write about my second "other mother," my dear neighbor, Mafalda Battistelli, or, as I called her, Zia Wa Wa. As a child, I could not pronounce Mafalda, and so called her Zia Wa Wa—Zia meaning aunt in Italian and Wa Wa was the only way I could pronounce Mafalda. She lived next door in what was many years

later to be called "The Italian House" by future owners. Her husband, Pasquale, we called Zio Pat —Zio meaning uncle in Italian and Pat was a shortened form of Pasquale. Linda and I were always welcome there. As I was a somewhat precocious child, and often considered a brat by some people, I wondered, as I grew up, how the Battistellis could be so nice to me! I always came to the back door, and upon seeing me, she would welcome me with a big smile and a hello and hug. She was the original "stay-at-home wife." She didn't drive, but was a wonderful cook and, sadly, was unable to have children.

Entering their kitchen, it was not unusual to see homemade pasta hanging from strings over the kitchen table. Zia Wa Wa was such a great cook—as well as being thoughtful and kind to Dad, Linda and me. When Mom was away several different times—either visiting her parents in Colorado, or once when she was in the hospital for surgery—we were invited over to their house for dinner. I remember some of these wonderful meals. Not being aware of the natural progression of courses in an Italian home, I filled up on the pasta course and was surprised to see the second course arrive, often roast chicken, and would wonder how I was going to get this down and still have room for dessert!

MY OTHER MOTHERS

Zio Pat was an architect with the U.S. Government, but also an artist and musician. He would often entertain us by sitting on the back stoop off of the kitchen and playing the mandolin while singing a rousing song. One song I remember was, "The Dark Town Strutter's Ball." That certainly would not be politically correct today. Pat was also talented on the violin and guitar. Their house had many artistic touches, such as crown molding on the ceiling, decorative molding surrounding the chandeliers in the living and dining rooms, and many of his own art-work, oil paintings, hanging on the walls.

Some of these paintings were of nude women, which prompted me to ask in my curious way, "Why don't they have clothes on?"

Zia Wa Wa would answer me calmly, as she responded to all of my questions, "Why, the human body is beautiful."

Well, this was a new concept for me to grasp at age six or seven!

In summer, Zia Wa Wa's mother, Mrs. Battillini, would often come to visit on the train from Philadelphia. Whereas Zia Wa Wa had black hair, wore no glasses, and was rather short and plump, her mother was a tall elegant lady. Her grey hair neatly coifed, she wore glasses and would be dressed in a longer-length dress and "old lady" black shoes with laces. We would sit on the screened-in porch on metal gliders, rocking back and forth, sipping ice-cold lemonade and chatting away the afternoon.

My favorite question for Zia Wa Wa would be, "How old are you?"
The answer was always the same, "Sixteen."

Another summer pastime I enjoyed with Zia Wa Wa was sitting to-gether on the cast-iron bench on the little flagstone patio in their shady back yard. Planted around the patio were colorful pansies. Of course there were other plants as well, whose names I no longer remember. Sit-ting there, we talked about flowers, gardens, trees and shrubs. These conversations helped spark my later interest in gardening.

Other times in colder weather I would visit on a late afternoon and we would lie on the thick carpeted living room floor listening to the ra-dio. Of course, I would ask why we were on the floor, and she would tell me that it was good for our backs. I remember one show, "The

17

Shadow," starring Lamont Cranston. The tagline was: "Who knows what evil lurks in the hearts of men? Only the Shadow knows."

There were other radio programs that we listened to, as I fondly remember those long-ago late afternoons, as the sun went down and we turned on the lights in their very formally decorated living room, while I lay on my back and gazed up at the crown molding on the ceiling.

During those years of my childhood, Zia Wa Wa would come to our house to visit my maternal grandmother, Lydia Brahmstadt, who was an invalid and lived in an in-law apartment attached to the back of our house. Grandma Brahmstadt left Boulder, Colorado, to come and live with us when I was seven. My grandfather had died, and later Grandma Brahmstadt had fallen and broken her hip. My mother and Zia Wa Wa would join my grandmother, and, as the three ladies chatted and gossiped about people in the neighborhood, I would hover nearby, sitting on a stool, hoping to add to my own informational list about the neighbors, and, in addition, perhaps learn juicy tidbits about pregnancy, childbirth and other topics of great interest to me. After repeated attempts to get rid of me—always failing—I remained a rapt listener.

I would bring over all of the neighborhood kids, one at a time, introducing them to the Battistellis. Soon they would also become welcome guests at the Battistelli home. As Zia Wa Wa and Zio Pat had no children of their own, I believe they really enjoyed these visits. Of course my friends all called them Zia Wa Wa and Zio Pat.

When the Battistellis' relatives visited from Bridgeport, Connecticut, we would socialize with their children. As a teenager, when their nephew, Eddie, was visiting by himself, I was invited to accompany them on day-long sightseeing trips in the Washington, D.C., area or on other fun excursions. Other similar invitations were often extended to me while I was growing up in my neighborhood. People with teenage visitors needed me to help entertain them. This sometimes worked to my advantage, as I was invited to some great parties where I met boys! Once I was invited to go on a trip through the Carolinas with a stop at Montreat, North Carolina, the home of the evangelist Billy

Graham. [The morning that I wrote about this trip to Montreat, Billy Graham had just died at the age of ninety-nine.]

As a teenager, I would return from dates, often spending extra time sitting in the boy's car, saying lengthy goodnights. Zia Wa Wa noticed this and, apparently concerned for my morality, mentioned this to my mother. She said that on different evenings I was seen in different cars with different boys. Mom, somewhat miffed at her comments, answered that she was happy I dated different boys and did not want me to "go steady." She also added that it was safer for me to be in front of our house in these cars instead of parked somewhere else. One of the popular parking spots during my growing-up years in Arlington was "watching the submarine races" at the Reflection Pool at the Mall in Washington. There were other spots, I am certain. So Zia Wa Wa continued to be concerned for me, as a mother would, into my teenage years.

I believe she helped fill in for my mother. Earlier in my childhood, my mother was busy caring for Linda as a newborn and later as a toddler. Zia Wa Wa took time to talk to me, listen to my stories, answer my many questions—really to be there for me.

I remember how I reacted to my sister's birth. I had been so excited to know that a new sister or brother was on the way. I told everyone I was going to have a baby sister. How this was a certainty in my four-and-a-half-year-old brain remains a mystery. But when Mom brought her home from the hospital, I quickly realized that she was not going to be the "instant playmate" that I had imagined. Mom was also very busy with this new baby, and I felt neglected. Being bumped from first place is always difficult. At this time, I must have started my visits to the Battistellis—where I was "mothered" by Zia Wa Wa. For this, I am grateful.

Later in life I experienced this pattern with my own children. I was overwhelmed with a new baby, my second child, Katy. Paul was a very active toddler and needed a lot of attention as well. He got this attention from my in-laws, May and Tim Clark. Paul loved visiting them. On Sunday evenings when they were driving him back to our house, Paul

19

would say, "No go home. No go home." So they filled in as parents for him when I was too busy or too tired.

Getting back to the Battistellis, while I was away at college, I would always go to visit them when I came home. Again, I was always welcome. Later, their happy faces appear in my wedding photos, joining the smiling faces of my Godmother, Aunt Sis, and her husband DeEarle, in the crowd of friends at our reception.

The very last time I visited the Battistellis, I had just returned from living in Switzerland. I had flown down from Boston with little Paul, aged seventeen months. He would toddle around in Mom's kitchen which had a large glass door facing the Battistelli house. He had blond curls and that chubby little face that most toddlers have. Zia Wa Wa could see Paul from her house. She adored Paul and could not stop saying how beautiful he was. One year later, Mom and Dad sold their house in Arlington Forest, the house I grew up in, and the house where I had an "other mother" next door. Sadly, two years later, Zia Wa Wa died. Pat lived there alone for a few more years, and then moved back to Bridgeport, Connecticut, to be with his brother's family, the family who used to visit with their teenage children.

As I got older, I would ask Mom if she ever missed her family in Crete, Nebraska. "Oh God, no! Why would anyone want to go back to Crete!" She also told me that she wanted to raise us without interference from family. Well, she succeeded.

MY OTHER MOTHERS

CRETE, NEBRASKA

How did Mom and Dad meet? Mom's family was of German descent. Her dad operated the grain elevator in Crete. Although she was born on a farm in Hallam, Nebraska, later the family, which then included a younger sister, Esther, moved to Crete. Dad's family was of Czech and German descent. His mom was divorced and working as a nurse, and so Dad's aunt and uncle, the Homolkas, raised him. At age fourteen, Dad ran away and joined the Army. He did this with a friend, both boys looking older than their age, and succeeded for a year until their actual age was discovered. I have the telegram the Army sent to his mother when he was sent back on a train to Crete.

Dad then entered Crete High School to complete his education. But he had missed a year and so entered sophomore year older than his classmates. Mom told me that he saw her walking down the hall and went home and told his aunt that he had seen the girl he was going to marry! He was three years older than Mom.

Dad graduated from high school, but was too poor to afford college. The high-school principal realized Dad was a quick learner and so over the next few years tutored him and helped him to prepare for the exam to apply to the U.S. Naval Academy. This was Dad's only opportunity for a college education. He was accepted into the Class of 1930. Although Mom was quite pretty and seemed to have many boyfriends, she must have seen Dad as "a rising star" and she waited for him.

So she went to "June Week" at the Academy in 1930 where she fell in love with the trees on the trolley ride from Washington to Annapolis. That is the story behind why I was so lucky to be born in Washington, grow up in Arlington, and to have lived a wonderful life.

LIFE IN THE FIFTH GRADE

My third "other mother" was my fifth-grade teacher, Miss (Maxine) Gold, later to become Mrs. Aarons.

At this point I want to mention my elementary-school years. I was too young to enter the first grade at the public school in our neighborhood, Kate Waller Barrett School. The cutoff rule was that I had to be age six by early September. Since I had a November birthday, I could not start school. Mom was desperate at this point that I should be in school. She was so determined, in fact, that she even tried to enroll me in the local Catholic school, St. Thomas More. This was desperation in its extreme, as Mom did not think much of the Catholic Church. But St. Thomas More School couldn't take me, as they were overcrowded. These were the years after the war, when the "baby boomers" were all entering school. Technically, I was not a "boomer" as I had been born in 1941. Mom's last chance was to enroll me in a private school for first grade, the Congressional School in Arlington. I hated it. It was pure torture, as it was run like a military school. Each day we were made to march single-file down the hall to the lunch room. We were not allowed to talk.While seated at long tables for lunch, we were also not allowed to talk. I was kept after school for "supervised play" on the playground, and was brought home much later in the day on a school bus, the last kid to be dropped off! Looking back, there were probably a large number of problem children there. I did not consider myself to be in that category.

Paul Robinson

per 1925 @ msn . com

Fortunately, as second grade appeared on the horizon, I was able to enter the public school, the Kate Waller Barrett School. I thought that I had died and gone to Heaven! As the Barrett School was also over-crowded, it had both morning and afternoon sessions that year. I was in the afternoon session. This enabled me to play outdoors all morning with the neighborhood kids, have lunch with Mom and then walk to school. By the time I was in fifth grade, I was riding my bike to school and sometimes coming home for lunch.

Looking back, I think that Mom was not as overjoyed as I was about the half-day sessions and my eating lunch at home. The Barrett School was located at the border of our neighborhood, and across the street from the school was the beginning of the Buckingham Apartment Complex I mentioned earlier. Today the original part of the school, built in the late 1930s and facing Henderson Road North, looks like it did when I walked through the front door for the first time in second grade. A red brick building with high windows, the original school looks like the school Ralphie attends in the film, *A Christmas Story*. The newer wing of the school is more modern with its entrance on the corner of Henderson Road North and North George Mason Drive.

The teachers I had for the first few years were pleasant enough, and I passed each grade successfully. By fifth grade I was fortunate to have Miss Gold as a teacher. She was beautiful, tall and elegant with a porce-lain complexion, green eyes the color of jade, and wavy jet-black hair. To my ten-year-old budding sense of fashion, I thought the bright-col-ored flowing scarves around her neck, rich jewel-toned dresses or sweaters with black skirts she wore were the epitome of haute couture. She was Jewish and I later learned that she had graduated from Mary Washington College, where eventually I was to enroll in 1959. There were few Jewish students when I entered Mary Washington, and I can imagine how socially challenging it might have been for Maxine Gold to study there.

So why was Miss Gold like another mother to me? At ten years old I was at a very awkward and gawky age. I was taller than most of the other kids, and was often asked "How's the weather up there?" It was extremely hurtful. We also had gym classes with mats on the gym floor where we were learning to tumble, stand on our heads and perform other body gyrations that were impossible for me to do. Seeing my predicament, Miss Gold would often hold onto my feet so that I could stand on my head, if only for a few seconds. She noticed my distress and was willing to help me out. At this age I was entering puberty and sometimes while at school I would feel queasy. I often wanted to go home. Miss Gold seemed to understand this and my mother was called to pick me up. I also had a bad complexion, since acne had suddenly appeared on my face. Facing challenging times, Miss Gold had my back.

I was a chatterbox. Miss Gold would announce near the end of the school day that if anyone talked during the last ten minutes, they would be kept after school. I was frequently "caught in the net" of chatterers. Was I angry to have to stay after? No. I believed Miss Gold was fair and followed-up on her warnings.

I remember recess where we went outdoors in the area behind the school. There was a lot of open space with some paved areas for the girls to play hopscotch and jump rope. The boys would run around the field playing war games or informal sessions of softball. I would spend this time with my two best friends, Linda Taylor and Jeanette Losee.

Besides jump rope and hopscotch, we spent a lot of time standing around and giggling. What would we talk about? We discussed the usual things: the other kids in the class; boys; gym class, and whether or not we would get picked first or last for the volleyball games; the bike rides we would go on over the weekend; and Jeanette's older and brainy brother, David. And I am sure we made fun among ourselves of some of the kids in our class. Some of our talk centered on the square dances held in the school gym several times a month. I was so tall that no one would dance with me except a boy named Albert—over the years, I have forgotten his last name! He was the same height as I was—possibly, even taller. He had transferred to Barrett from another school that had closed. This school was in a less-desirable part of Arlington and so the students who entered our school were often not as fortunate as we were. Albert was actually fourteen years old and in the sixth grade. So my choices were limited.

We girls weren't averse to gossip. This was before the days of cyber-bullying, but we just talked and giggled among ourselves, discussing classmates we thought were odd. One boy ran around the playground at recess, both arms extended on either side, pretending to be an airplane. He did this almost every day, totally alone, and making airplane noises the entire time. There were other kids we thought were strange, and I know we must have discussed them. I had a small, black "Brownie" camera. I have photos of Linda, Jeanette and me on the playground and one photo of Miss Gold with her hair blowing in the breeze, standing off to the side and watching us.

I honestly do not remember much of what I learned during those years at Kate Waller Barrett Elementary School. It is a blur. I must have learned enough to be promoted each year. But fifth grade was different. It was exciting. It was the year of Queen Elizabeth's coronation in London. I vividly remember the discussions, the pictures we brought into class cut out from *Life Magazine*, and the scrapbooks all of us made of those pictures. This made a profound impression on my ten-year-old mind and emotions. I developed a great interest and love of all things British which continues to this day. When I first visited London in 2001, I toured Westminster Abbey. Walking around this magnificent edifice with Kelly, my daughter-in-law, seeing the famous tombs of illustrious kings, queens, playwrights, and authors, we met a docent who walked along with us. She told us that she was there for the coronation as a young girl, probably aged ten, standing outside with her mother, watching as the young queen entered the enormous front doors. The docent then pointed out the seats where Churchill, the American representative and other world leaders sat for the ceremony. So, Miss Gold sparked this interest in fifth grade which continues today.

Between fifth and sixth grade Miss Gold got married. She returned to teach our sixth-grade class as Mrs. Aarons. I was overjoyed to have her as a teacher for my last year at the Barrett school. I was so happy to have her as my teacher again, that I asked Mom if she could invite the

25

Aarons for dinner. They probably didn't realize what an honor this was, as I had never wanted any other teacher to come to dinner. I remember that we had fish and the dinner seemed to go quite well; conversation flowing at a good and comfortable pace. Sometime after that, Mrs. Aarons announced to our class that she was "expecting." Lucky for her and her husband, but not so lucky for us. Because she was in this condition, she was unable to continue teaching for the last half of our sixth-grade year. Yes, in the 1950s, teachers could not keep their positions past a certain time in their pregnancy. Sadly, she left us. We then had a man teacher, Mr. McBride. He seemed nice enough, but how could he possibly replace Mrs. Aarons! He was also a Mormon and would talk to us about the evils of alcohol, smoking and even drinking Coca-Cola. Well, I had already made up my own mind about all of this since Dad was a heavy smoker, and both of my parents were social drinkers and even offered me small sips of their cocktails on occasion. Of course, everyone drank Coke. So, poor Mr. McBride's advice fell on "deaf ears" as far as I was concerned.

I left sixth grade and the Barrett School and my favorite teacher, Mrs. Aarons. I moved on to Wakefield High School which I attended until I graduated as a senior in 1959. But news of Mrs. Aarons continued to flow in through my best friend, Linda (another "Linda"). Her mother worked at Garfinkel's Department Store in Arlington. Mrs. Aarons would come in to shop occasionally over the next ten years, and would stop and chat with my friend's mother. We learned she had two boys, and unfortunately, one had a serious health issue. At one time she lived in the Buckingham apartments across the street from our school. Perhaps she moved into a larger home with her expanding family, but I believe she remained in Arlington. I would like to think that she was as wonderful a mother to her boys as she was a wonderful "other mother" for me. As I lost contact with her after sixth grade, Mrs. Aarons' smiling face does not appear in my wedding photos.

My Other Mothers

My Five Other Mothers

My godmother and namesake, Christine Logsdon, whom I called Aunt Sis, on her "farm" with her pheasants. Her husband DeEarle and my father were classmates at the Naval Academy. Aunt Sis helped me survive summer camp when I was ten years old. As a teenager, I remember a wonderful weekend in the country with Mom, Aunt Sis, Linda, and a close girlfriend. Aunt Sis was part of a group of friends who gave me a bridal shower the summer before I got married. Her smiling face appears in my wedding photos.

Above: My second "other mother," my dear neighbor, Mafalda Battistelli, or as I called her, Zia Wa Wa, and her husband, Pasquale, whom I called Zio Pat—"Aunt and Uncle."

Left: Zia Wa Wa and me in my backyard.

When Mom was away several different times—either visiting her parents in Colorado, or once when she was in the hospital for surgery—we were invited over to their house for wonderful meals. I spent a lot of time in the Battistelli home and received some much needed support and advice.

My third "other mother" was my fifth-grade teacher, Miss (Maxine) Gold, later to become Mrs. Aarons. At ten years old I was at a very awkward and gawky age. I was taller than most of the other kids—and Mrs. Aarons was the one who helped me cope with this difficult time and helped me feel good about myself.

My fourth "other mother" was a Navy wife, Arlene Ostrander.

Pictured above, we were at Nags Head on the Outer Banks in North Carolina—I'm on the right wearing the straw hat and Arlene is next to me in the checkered bathing suit.

I met Arlene three years earlier, when I spent the summer with my Aunt Essie and Uncle John at White Sands Proving Grounds, in New Mexico—and Arlene took me under her wing, knowing I was a teenager far away from home, and helped me feel comfortable and enjoy my trip.

And here is my fifth "other mother"— my high-school French teacher at Wakefield High School, Mrs. Anne Lanpher. Her enthusiasm for all things French was contagious, and she comforted me when I was very apprehensive about my mother's surgery. Although I thought I was a sophisticated senior, I learned that I still needed a "mother" to comfort me.

MY PARENTS

My mother, Helen Dorner.

To the left: Her graduation from high school in Crete, Nebraska.

Below: Just married, 1933.

My mother was loving and caring and I have nothing but fond memories. There were times, as I was to experience when I became a mother, when the pressures of life on her necessitated brief respites— during which I found help from "other mothers."

My dad, Edward Dorner.

Above: A high school football star in Crete, Nebraska.

To the left: His graduation from the U.S. Naval Academy.

Dad was a perfect match for Mom; they were both wonderful parents to Linda and me. Also, it was amazing how often Dad's Naval Academy classmates figured prominently in our lives.

CHILDHOOD

Above left: Dad, Mom and me—in 1942, on the way to my Christening at Glen Carlyn Episcopal Church.

Above right: All dressed up for Easter—Mom and Dad in our backyard before we went to Easter dinner at a hotel dining room.

Right: Me, Grandma Brahmstadt (Mom's mother) and Linda, visiting in her apartment which was attached to our house at 113 North Columbus Street in Arlington, Virginia— pictured here with snow!

With Linda.

Above: Sitting on our front steps in 1949.

Left and Right: Halloween in 1950.

I was a stickler; every one of my costumes had to be just perfect! I don't remember why Linda isn't in costume; but note her ever-present hair bow.

*At Linda's birthday party at our house in 1950.
There's me, always the "big boss," sitting regally in
the chair, while the guest of honor, Linda, is to the
right, wearing her signature hair bow.*

Out in the world.

Left: On my way to second grade at the Kate Waller Barrett School.
With me is my neighbor, Chris Hanburger, who lived across the street. Chris was a football star in high school and college and went on to a Hall of Fame career with the Washington Redskins. I have no idea what I'm staring at—maybe another friend.

Below: At age nine, getting ready to head out to Camp High Road with Chip Logsdon, who was six. He was the son of Christine Logsdon, my first "other mother." That's our family Oldsmobile.

In the Battistelli backyard. Home of my second "other mother," Mafalda Battistelli and her husband Pasquale—"Zia" and "Zio" to me.

At left: That's me at age twelve.

Lower left: Mom—and you can just see that it's the same wrought-iron bench, a style popular then.

Lower right: Dear Zio Pat, who loved his yard and garden and was so nice to me.

School Days

These were when I was 11 to 13 years old.

Above: All dressed up and ready to go out— Linda and me.

Right: I'm between Jean and Sally Hilger, in our neighborhood in 1952.

39

On the playground.

*Left: Me with my friend
Jeanette Losee.*

Below: Linda and Jeanette.

*We must have taken turns
with our camera.*

With my great friend, Linda Taylor.
Notice my handwriting with curlicues. And look
at our saddle shoes—very stylish!
Across the street is the Buckingham Apartment
complex—part of the historic
garden-apartment movement,
popularized in part by Eleanor Roosevelt.

41

HIGH SCHOOL

Hanging out.

Above: I'm second from right, as my friends and I are off to lunch. Notice that we're dressed for the occasion—it was a more formal era.

Right: Still dressed up! I'm on the right, with my friends in our "rec room." Notice the knotty-pine paneling and the knick-knacks adorning the wall.

*Tom and Tom.
Neither was the Tom
I would marry.*

*Above: My junior-year
boyfriend, Tom Terry, whom I
met in typing class where he
was the only boy with 12 girls.
We're sitting on the Battistelli
stone wall. He was one of the
boys whom Aunt Zia
"watched carefully."*

*Right: My senior-prom date,
Tom Pachler, and me. We
weren't serious, but I have to
admire a guy who looks so
lovingly at his date.*

"Sitting on the dock of the bay—sitting in the morning sun—sitting when the evening comes."

With apologies to Otis Redding, this was actually the dock on the lake, at our family summer place.

Above: Two unidentified kids having fun.

Left: Linda relaxing in the sun.

We had great times there— and I especially remember the dinner with Mom and Aunt Sis, where the talk turned to dating experiences and I felt grown-up for the first time.

MY OTHER MOTHERS

First Flight!
Here I am on the tarmac, getting ready to take my first flight—all
by myself—returning home to Washington, D.C., after visiting Aunt
Essie in Norfolk, Virginia. The plane was a twin-engine DC-3.
Today the DC-3 is one of the aircraft on display in the
National Air and Space Museum in Washington, D.C.
Each time I see it there, I remember my first flight
and feel rather old.

Aunt Essie and Uncle John.

Left: Clowning around a bit, while helping us at our house in Arlington.

Below: Uncle John, dressed slightly differently, on duty at the White Sands Proving Ground.

New Mexico.

During the summer when I was fourteen-and-a-half, I traveled to visit Aunt Essie [left] and Uncle John at the White Sands Proving Grounds where Uncle John was stationed.

Below: The Ostranders, friends of Aunt Essie and Uncle John.

My fourth "other mother," Arlene Ostrander, is standing in the center.

MY WEDDING

My godmother and "other mother" Christine Logsdon is on the left, with my mother on the right. It looks like they're at some sort of house reception in Arlington—it may have had something to do with my wedding.

Below: At my wedding reception at the Fort Myer Officers Club; my "other mother," Zia We Wa, is standing at center, holding the black purse.

FULL CIRCLE

In 1932, my mother did an extraordinary thing for the times. She left her home in Colorado and took a train to Los Angeles. Dad was there and Mom was determined to be close to him until they were married. Mom moved in with her future mother-in-law, my grandmother, Frances Dorner, and with Dad's very young sister, Edith—who was to become my aunt. After spending a year in Los Angeles, Mom took the train to Yuma, Arizona where she and Dad were married by a Justice of the Peace. That was February 18, 1933. They were married forty-six years at the time of Dad's passing in 1979.

Above and Right: Frances Dorner was a nurse, working at Los Angeles Memorial Hospital.

49

In a notable turn of events, Mom realized that young Edith, who was in the third grade, needed some support. Frances was working a lot and Edith lacked proper clothes for school. So Mom, who had homemaking talent, got to work and sewed several dresses for Edith. Mom was also a great cook and prepared many delicious meals for Edith.
I met with Edith years later, and I was so touched to realize that Mom had been "another mother" to Edith.

Above: In a photo from the 1930s, from the left: Mom, her sister Aunt Essie and Dad's little sister Edith, who became my aunt when Mom and Dad married.

Right: In 1932, Mom and Edith in Los Angeles

My Other Mothers

You're in the Navy Now

My fourth "other mother" was Arlene Ostrander, a Navy wife.

At age fourteen-and-a-half, I spent the summer with my Aunt Essie and Uncle John at White Sands Proving Ground, in New Mexico.

Uncle John was a naval officer working at White Sands with the guided-missile program. I had this great opportunity offered to me. I had already done some traveling alone, but mostly within the state of Virginia. I had visited Aunt Essie in Norfolk and although I had been dropped off there by Mom and Dad in their car, I took my first flight ever from Norfolk to Washington all by myself. I can still remember standing on the airstrip in Norfolk with my Aunt and quivering with apprehension before the flight. Aunt Essie asked me why I was so nervous. I didn't have a logical answer. I just was!

The plane I was about to board was a twin-engine DC-3. Today the DC-3 is one of the aircraft on display in the National Air and Space Museum in Washington, D.C. Each time I see it there, I remember my first flight and feel rather old.

But returning to my upcoming trip to White Sands. It seemed like a good idea when I received the invitation; but as the trip loomed closer, I began to have second thoughts. Beset with apprehension, I boarded the four-engine plane and headed west. At age fourteen-and-a-half, I was traveling alone. I had to change flights in Dallas/Fort Worth and board another plane for El Paso—where my aunt and uncle would meet me. As I disembarked and headed through the terminal, I saw cowboys—

yes, real cowboys—wearing cowboy boots and ten-gallon hats. They were standing around and casually leaning against the walls of the terminal. Once I had secured my luggage at baggage claim, we set out on the hour-and-a-half trip out to White Sands, riding in Uncle John's yellow Chrysler convertible. Soon we were cruising along at one hundred miles an hour, with the top down, my hair blowing in the wind as the sage brush flew by. I had arrived—really arrived, in the great Southwest.

Life settled down as I became familiar with my new routine. I was left alone for much of the day, as Aunt Essie worked as a medical secretary at the military dispensary on post. Uncle John was busy with the guided-missile program every day and occasionally these missiles were tested. (More on this later in the story.) But at noon each day, I was expected to show up at home and join my aunt and uncle for lunch. Lunch was usually filling but easy to prepare; I remember some sort of meat—sandwiches, cold cuts or hot dogs, maybe potato salad—but we always had cucumbers. Today when I eat cucumbers, I think of those lunches. Part of the lunch routine was my uncle grilling me on my activities for each day. "Who were you with? Where are you going? When will you be home?" I was unaccustomed to this strict military discipline! Looking back on that summer, I am sure they were both concerned with the responsibility of having me there. After all, they had no children of their own. And I was a teenager. Even scarier.

While visiting my aunt and uncle in White Sands, I was able to meet their friends, all other naval officers and their wives, and in some cases their children. Part of their social circle were the Ostranders, Commander Max Ostrander, his wife Arlene, and their three boys—Larry, Mike and Butch. Therefore, my fourth "other mother" was Arlene Ostrander, a Navy wife. She and her husband were best friends with my aunt and uncle. I became friends with their three boys. Larry was about my age; Mike was twelve; and Butch was nine. Somehow Mike became my "pal." It must have been his quirky sense of humor or the comfort level we shared. So, most mornings I spent roaming around the post with the Ostrander boys—more often with Mike. Afternoons we walked to the post swimming pool in one-hundred-degree heat which never seemed to bother us, as it was so dry. I remember wearing blue jeans and a white shirt tied in a knot at my waist and probably sneakers. We stayed at the pool most afternoons, horsing around and trying to keep cool in the water. So my friendship with the boys meant that I became close to their mom. She always welcomed me as part of her family and, as they had a piano in the living room, she invited me to play it whenever I was there. Arlene told me a little bit about her background. She graduated from Purdue University in Indiana. After graduation she worked for Calvert Whiskey in Baltimore, Maryland. I was surprised when she told me that part of her job was being a "taster." When I asked her how she could do this every day, she laughed and told me that she didn't swallow, but spit it out. Well, just like a wine-tasting event! While working in Baltimore, she must have met Max. He was either still at the Naval Academy in Annapolis, not far from Baltimore, or he had already graduated and was stationed nearby. I can't remember the details. Many evenings our two families had cookouts together, enjoying grilling steaks or burgers and probably finishing our meals with "s'mores" for dessert.

On several mornings, Arlene took me to watch the guided-missile tests. In 1956 the Navy was testing the Talus Missile, a tactical missile. These tests were not always successful and the whole thing had to be scrapped. But when they were successfully deployed—what excitement—an ear-splitting boom and behind it a burst of flame as the missiles gradually ascended into the sky!

One late afternoon our two families drove out to the White Sands National Monument. We had a cookout and the boys and I sledded down the sand dunes on blankets. What fun. This was 1956 and the sand dunes were not yet protected as a national monument.

Another weekend our two families drove to Ruidoso, a town in the southern part of the state, located in the cool pines of Lincoln County, and famous for its race track, Ruidoso Downs. We were staying at a private home there which belonged to friends of my aunt and uncle. The plan was that we could stay there because their friends were away and not using the house. What a beautiful home—a large ranch-style with enough bedrooms for all of us. We had dinner, listened to Nat King Cole 78-rpm records on their phonograph, and were settling in nicely for our next two nights in the house. Then—surprise! The owners showed up. Something got lost in the translation of the invitation. I never learned what the problem was. The next two nights I shared a bed with their teenage daughter. She had married a jockey from the race track and I believe had a baby who was not with her that weekend. Well, this was a completely different and unusual lifestyle from what I had experienced at this point in my life. I was uncomfortable. Arlene noticed my mood and talked to me about my discomfort with this unusual weekend. She was a mother, after all, and she could sense what my Aunt was unable to see. After Arlene talked to me, I was able to enjoy the rest of our time there. We went to the races and later drove around this beautiful resort town in New Mexico. I also remember my uncle making pancakes for breakfast on one of the mornings we were there. He made them in different animal shapes. That was unusual, and they tasted delicious.

I spent about six weeks in White Sands. The night I left we had a cookout, again with the Ostranders. I went to bed early that night, since I had to get up at three a.m. for my return flight to Washington, D.C. My Aunt and Uncle drove me through the dark night to the airport at El Paso, where I boarded the plane for my trip home; but I do not remember the return trip—it was a blur. During the next few years the Ostranders were stationed in both Philadelphia, Pennsylvania, and Norfolk, Virginia. I introduced them to Mom and Dad, and they had a good time socializing, as Dad and Max were both Naval Academy graduates. Once again, the Naval Academy connection came into play. Later, when I was seventeen, our family drove to Nags Head, North Carolina, in the Outer Banks. Arlene and the boys drove down from Norfolk, and we spent the day at the beach. The rip tide there is treacherous and although warning signs had been posted, one of the boys almost drowned. Thankfully, he was rescued by a lifeguard and survived.

The last news of the Ostranders I just learned from my sister, Linda. She remembered visiting our aunt and uncle in Oxnard, California, and met Max and Arlene at that time. Both Max and my uncle had since retired from the Navy. For many years I received Christmas cards from the Ostranders, always with a little note about the family. I also sent cards with my news. One year, the cards stopped. Then the second year —still no cards. The next year I received a note from Larry that both of his parents were deceased. How sad to learn that one of my "other mothers" was gone. How lucky I was, though, to have had her in my life that summer in New Mexico, when I was fourteen-and-a-half, so many years ago.

CHRISTINE CLARK

TEENAGE YEARS

I look back on my teenage years as some of the happiest in my life. Why is this? So many teens are miserable during this time. Perhaps my memories are distorted and I am blanking out the bad times. But I can hardly remember the bad—only the feelings of life being the best I could imagine. My worries could be narrowed down to just a few: The first was that the Russians would drop the bomb—remember this was the height of the Cold War—and we had air raids in school where we would file down into the basement and line up quietly along the lockers in the hallway. The other worry was that I might not pass Algebra or Chemistry. I had looked forward to high school during my last few years at Barrett Elementary School. I would watch the high-school girls getting off the bus carrying their books. They looked so self-assured and happy with their lives. I couldn't wait to join this elite sisterhood. Today I also realize that this was a time in my life when I really had no worries, as I had a stable home life, meals appeared on the table with simple regularity, family vacations were planned, and, in fact, I had absolutely no responsibilities except to get through high school with grades good enough to be accepted into college.

Mom and Dad opened our home to my friends. Mom encouraged me to have parties. I remember my fifteenth birthday party. We were going to a dance at Wakefield, my high school. Before the dance, Mom had me invite my date and my girlfriends and their dates to our house where she had prepared a delicious dinner. There we sat, all of us, around our dining room table, acting like young adults. After dinner, various other parents arrived to drive us to the dance. There were other parties during those years which were as memorable. Years later at my fiftieth high school reunion, classmates came up to me and told me how they remembered being invited to our house and that my parents were so friendly and the house looked so nice!

Wakefield High School was built in 1953. It was a state-of-the-art school located in south Arlington. The other high school was Washington and Lee, located in north Arlington. It was overcrowded and thus the need for another high school. Our class entered in 1953 as seventh graders and were the only class to go through Wakefield for six years, graduating in 1959. Perhaps my six years there created the loyalty which still exists today, as I attend class reunions, alumni events, and just recently a celebration of the school's sixtieth birthday. Those years were truly happy.

Mom also was an excellent social planner. She quietly but unwaveringly got Linda and me into dance classes, cotillions, and eventually on the debutante circuit. The cotillions I especially enjoyed were the Army-Navy-Air Force Cotillions held at the Fort Myer Officers Club. I was sixteen and seventeen when I attended these dances. I was required to bring in three presentable young men with me to be on the "floor committee."

During those years, Mom spent hours on the telephone calling mothers of eligible boys to get them on the list of the floor committee. We girls wore formal gowns, long white gloves, and had dance cards which were filled throughout the evening. The boys were required to wear a tuxedo or military uniform if they were in any of the military academies—West Point, the Naval Academy, Air Force Academy or Coast Guard Academy. We were also required to go through a receiving line consisting of military officers and their wives. There were live bands playing at these dances. We could also bring a date—sometimes a college boy and, in my case, a boyfriend from Yale who will appear later in this story.

I also attended tea dances at the Naval Academy on Sunday afternoons. Sometimes I went to these with high-school girlfriends and other times Dad drove me down to Annapolis. These dances were held in Bancroft Hall and were for Plebes—first-year students, or freshmen. The purpose was for the Plebes to meet girls, dance and socialize. Mom signed me up for these as well. Later, during my college years, I attended Sunday afternoon dances at Fort Belvoir, where we would dance with the ROTC men who had just completed their summer courses.

I remember one dance where the ROTC cadets spontaneously broke into song, "We're the rambling wreck from Georgia Tech." I would drive down to these dances with a friend, an older girl who had already graduated from college and was seriously husband-hunting. She was successful and eventually married one of the men she met at these dances. Her mother was forever grateful to Mom for getting us on the list to attend the Fort Belvoir Sunday dances.

My Other Mothers

La Vie Français

My last "other mother" was my high-school French teacher, Mrs. Anne Lanpher. The summer before I entered my junior year, I met Tom Terry while attending typing school. Tom was the only boy in the class of twelve girls. He soon became my boyfriend. As our friendship grew,

Tom told me a friend of his parents had just been hired to teach French at my school, Wakefield, and would start teaching that fall. Mrs. Lanpher was from Scotland and had met Tom's father while both were university students in France and had bicycled through the French countryside together.

Lucky me! On the first day of school I learned that Mrs. Lanpher was teaching third-year French and I was in her class! Because of a lack of classroom space, our class met in the second-floor auditorium lobby. I can still picture this room which had fieldstone walls and large windows overlooking the front of the school. There were free-standing bulletin boards, plastered with colorful posters of French scenes, such as Paris and the surrounding countryside. The blackboard, which was actually green, was also free-standing. Mrs. Lanpher was somewhere in her later forties or early fifties—or as the French say, "a woman of a certain age." Her silver-grey hair was cut short in a soft "do." She wore glasses and dressed in Scottish plaid skirts and soft colorful cashmere sweaters. Her enthusiasm for all things French was contagious. As our class was smaller with fewer third-year students taking French, a sense of "camaraderie" infused our group.

One Saturday morning Mrs. Lanpher invited our class to her home in south Arlington for a typical French breakfast of coffee and croissants. What fun. But more important was that she cared to give of herself both in time and energy. We had a chance to sample French food and also to meet her husband and her two sons. The next year, my senior year, she was my teacher for fourth-year French. That winter my mother had to have surgery. I was worried and apprehensive. On the day of Mom's surgery, as I climbed the stairs to our second-floor lobby classroom, Mrs. Lanpher was also walking up and immediately noticed my concern. She asked what was wrong, and, as I told her, she sympathized and said something comforting to help alleviate my worries. As it turned out, Mom recovered completely. Although I thought I was a very sophisticated senior, I learned that day that when I was worried, I still needed a "mother" to comfort me.

In 1959 I graduated from Wakefield High School and entered Mary Washington College in Fredericksburg, Virginia. Although my parents drove me around for the college search process to various women's colleges in Virginia—Sweet Briar, Hollins and Mary Baldwin to name a few—these were all private colleges and expensive. Dad could afford to send me to a state college, and thus it was to be Mary Washington. To be accepted, I had to have a good enough grade average from Wakefield, which I did. I also had to take the College Board exams. I did not perform as well as I could have. But being in the National Honor Society and French Honor Society, as well as being a member of the Wakefield Guides, must have helped get me accepted.

Located in Fredericksburg, Virginia, the college has a beautiful campus. It is adorned with red-brick buildings fronted with white columns, set among gently rolling hills, and planted with many beautiful trees. Springtime found the campus radiant with flowering dogwood and fruit trees, as well as many spring bulbs in bloom. It "reeked of Southern charm." Another plus—although it was a state college, girls from many other states besides Virginia attended, as well as some students from other countries. So in its own way, it was somewhat cosmopolitan. Social life was possible as there were various military bases such as Quantico and Fort Belvoir nearby. The University of Virginia was a few hours away in Charlottesville, and other men's colleges dotted the surrounding area. It was also about an hour's drive from Washington which offered many cultural and social opportunities, as well as other universities such as Georgetown. I graduated from Mary Washington in 1963 with a bachelor's degree in French.

In my senior year, I married Tom Clark in a military wedding at the Fort Myer Chapel in Arlington. Tom was a lieutenant in the United States Army Corps of Engineers. At the time of our wedding, he was stationed in Berlin, Germany, as a helicopter pilot. We wanted to marry at Christmas time, and we both wanted a military wedding. My sister, Linda, was my maid of honor. Joseph Hughes, also an army officer and one of Tom's oldest friends, was his best man. We walked out of the chapel under an arch of swords and rode to our reception at the Officers Club in a horse-drawn carriage. All very romantic!

But I must return for a while to my years at Wakefield and Anne Lanpher as a favorite teacher and "other mother." Anne Lanpher appears in my wedding photos, smiling and standing alongside my godmother, Christine Logsdon, her husband DeEarle, and my neighbor, Mafalda Battistelli and her husband, Pat. A year after our wedding, Tom and I attended Tom Terry's wedding in the Chapel at Jonathan Edwards College at Yale University. The Lanphers were there as guests, and I had a nice long catch-up chat with Anne. This was the last time I saw her. Tom and I moved to Switzerland the following summer. Anne's husband died some years later and she eventually moved into an assisted-living facility in Washington, D.C. A classmate, Marion Stewart Emerson, kept in touch with her, visiting her frequently. Anne died about ten years afterward. Thus, sadly I lost yet another "other mother."

Another teacher I had for Speech, Mrs. Willingham, was so very committed to teaching that she took the entire class on a field trip one Sunday morning to her Protestant church in Washington, D.C. The purpose of the trip was to hear her pastor's sermon, as she thought he exemplified great skill in public speaking. She also brought us to American University, again in Washington, to produce a radio program in the studio of their Communications Department. Today whenever I hear the waltz from "Swan Lake"—which was the show's background music—I remember the days we spent there producing that program.

But while a student at Wakefield, I had other teachers—both men and women—who were so very dedicated not only in their professionalism but also in their ability to bring enthusiasm and excitement to the subjects they taught. But in my story, I mention only the women, as this is about women who acted as "other mothers" to me. These women teachers taught us how to behave, how to treat others and how to cope with the many emotional and physical stresses of our teen years.

Our Dean of Students for Girls, Mrs. Mare, was in charge of the Wakefield Guides. There was a rigorous application process involved, as we applicants had to be approved by all of our teachers for this position, since we would be missing class time to take foreign visitors around our school, often joining them for lunch in the school cafeteria. I passed the application process and became a Guide. These visitors, both men and women, came from countries throughout the world. Wakefield was the only high school they would visit as part of their tour of the United States. I remember one visitor, a charming man from Hong Kong, whom I joined for lunch in the school cafeteria after our tour. He gave me a pair of mother-of-pearl earrings with an Asian design. I wore those earrings for years, until I eventually lost them. (I keep losing jewelry!)

Mrs. Mare taught us how to be conversational, at ease and gracious with these guests. She also taught us how to ask appropriate questions about their various countries. I remember several evenings when the Guides were bussed into the city to attend receptions at the International Center, where we mingled with these foreign visitors, chatting with them while munching on cookies and sipping punch.

Mrs. Mare gave us a course in diplomacy and manners. I was, indeed, fortunate to have so many "other mothers" as teachers during my six years at Wakefield High School.

My Other Mothers

Nothing prepares us to be a mother. Some women have had earlier experiences with children such as babysitting, being an older sister in a large family and helping raise the younger children, being trained in early-childhood education, or other various experiences with young children. But I believe we are all "beginners" with our own children. I had always wanted to get married and have children—but only two! Having grown up with one sister, I thought this was what I wanted for myself. Because I got married so young and had both of my children by the time I was twenty-five, I often felt unprepared for the job!

I took a Red Cross course on infant care in Boston at the Jordan Marsh department store. I read numerous books on baby care. My "Bible" on the subject was Dr. Spock's book, *Baby and Child Care*. When I had my first child in Switzerland, Dr. Spock was my go-to source for everything, as some child-care practices in Switzerland in 1964 were totally different from what we were doing in the United States. But I was really "flying by the seat of my pants." Tom was extremely supportive and helpful at the time. He encouraged me and backed my decisions on how to care for our firstborn. He also relieved me on many Saturdays so that I could take the train into Zurich for a day of shopping, strolling along the Limmat River, having lunch in a restaurant, and returning by late afternoon. Tom was also "ahead of his time" in that he became involved in caring for our baby. Very quickly, he became adept at diaper changing and feeding baby Paul.

Slowly, painstakingly, I learned to care for our son as I became more comfortable in my new "mother role." After having our second child, Katy, who was born in Boston, my mother came to help me the first few weeks at home.

I will always remember as I was changing a diaper or bathing my daughter, my mother saying, "Well, you know what you are doing."

"Yes, Mom," I replied, "I learned to do this in Switzerland."

Mom was a good mother. But having my own children with all of the demands on time and energy, I finally understood why Mom was not always available to me—either physically or emotionally. Like Mom, I had to depend on other people to help care for my children. I hired a babysitter once a week, so that I could get away to shop, swim at the Y, or just drive somewhere for some "alone time." As I mentioned earlier, my in-laws were always there to help out by taking Paul or Katy when I needed to go out or travel with Tom. My parents also drove up from the D.C. area to visit and share "child sitting" with my in-laws when Tom and I went on vacations or business trips.

During the time the children were very young, Tom and I went to church separately, each staying home with the children while the other was in church. I can remember going the small Episcopal church in our town and, after the service was over, wanting to get in the car and drive somewhere—anywhere, and just keep driving and not return home until much later in the day! Of course, I didn't do this.

I grew into my role as a mother. As my children got older, I enjoyed them more. By the time they were teenagers, I totally enjoyed being a mother. Looking back, I remember Mom seemed to savor those years in our lives as well.

Today, because I do understand the stresses of motherhood that Mom experienced, I realize even more how important my "other mothers" were in my childhood and teenage years. They enriched my life—spending time with me, listening to me, or understanding me when I felt alone, uncomfortable, uncertain or anxious about something. They added another dimension to my life. They were role models for the woman I would become. I believe many women have shared my experience in some way. I hope they have had "other mothers" in their lives as I have.

I have been so very fortunate to have had my "other mothers" in my life—all of them.

Godmother, Neighbor, Teachers and Navy Wife.

Full Circle

Los Angeles, California — 1932

In February of 1932, Helen Brahmstadt, my mother, boarded the train in Boulder, Colorado, and left her family to go live in Los Angeles. My father was in Los Angeles living part-time with his mother, Frances Bartok Dorner. The Great Depression was impacting lives throughout the country. Dad had graduated from the Naval Academy in 1930. For various reasons, Dad was not commissioned as a naval officer. They had planned to marry then, but Dad did not have a job. By 1932 he was working as a land surveyor with the United States Coast and Geodetic Survey. He worked in Southern California in the Mojave Desert and in

Yuma, Arizona. Mom was a determined woman and knew she wanted to marry Dad, and so she left her family to be closer to him, as well as to find a new and exciting life on the West Coast.

She settled in comfortably with her future mother-in-law and eight year old Edith, Dad's much younger sister, where they lived in a modest bungalow with a small porch in front. The front yard was probably planted with various succulents such as agave, cactus, and maybe some rosemary—all growing rampant in the hot and sunny climate of Southern California. I can even imagine a eucalyptus tree or two growing in the backyard!

Frances Dorner was trained as a nurse, working in Los Angeles Memorial Hospital. Her reputation as a skilled nurse also enabled her to do a lot of private-duty nursing, sometimes for famous Hollywood movie stars. As a result, Edith was left alone a lot as a child, enjoying the freedom to roam the neighborhood and to play unsupervised—sometime a mixed blessing! (I say this in reference as a stark contrast to today's "helicopter parents.") Since Edith resembled the child actress, Shirley Temple, her mother was always entering her in Shirley Temple look-alike contests! Unfortunately, she never won. Mom told me much later how much she liked and respected her mother-in-law. Their relationship was close.

Years later I visited Edith in Davis, California. She was in her early 90s then. She told me how my mother filled in as a mother for her during that time. Edith was about to start third grade, but unfortunately had no dresses to wear, as her own mom was too busy working to provide Edith with appropriate clothes for school. My mother, with her domestic skills, immediately sewed several dresses for Edith. That year, Mom spent lots of time with Edith during the days when her mother was working. Mom was such a good cook and I know she must have prepared many delicious meals that year in Los Angeles. Several years later, after my parents were married and living in Washington, D.C., they invited Edith to come east and live with them, although this never happened.

When I did visit with Edith when she was much older, I was very touched and happy to hear her tell me those stories of long ago when my mother was "another mother" for her.

After spending a year in Los Angeles, Mom took the train to Yuma, Arizona, where she and Dad were married by a justice of the peace. This was February 18, 1933. They were married forty-six years at the time of Dad's passing in 1979.

And so, that little story about my mother helping young Edith all those many years ago—brings this full circle.

Mothers do their best. Help is often available. Children need love.

To all mothers—and to all "other mothers"—thank you.

ACKNOWLEDGEMENTS

Many thanks to Jack Shillingford, who has listened patiently to my stories and encouraged me to write about them.

Many thanks to my sister, Linda Lippner, who always helps me fill in the facts and events of our childhood with details I have forgotten.

Thanks to my "Pool Friends" at Foxfire in Naples, Florida, who encourage me to write and eagerly await my next story.

Thanks to Bernie Mendillo, without whose help this book would not be possible.

Finally, much thanks and gratitude to the all of the women who were my "other mothers."

CHRISTINE CLARK WAS BORN IN ARLINGTON, VIRGINIA. SHE GRADUATED FROM MARY WASHINGTON COLLEGE IN FREDERICKSBURG, VIRGINIA, IN 1963, WITH A B.A. IN FRENCH. SHE MARRIED THOMAS CLARK IN 1962. THEY LIVED IN BADEN, SWITZERLAND, BEFORE SETTLING IN CANTON, MASSACHUSETTS.

39004640R00046

Made in the USA
Middletown, DE
17 March 2019